A SCOTTISH ASSEMBLY

By the same author

Poetry
New Chatto Poets II (a contributor)
Sharawaggi (with W. N. Herbert)
Other Tongues:
Young Scottish Poets in English, Scots and Gaelic (editor)

Literary Criticism
The Savage and the City in the Work of T. S. Eliot
About Edwin Morgan (co-editor with Hamish Whyte)

A SCOTTISH
ASSEMBLY

Robert Crawford

Chatto & Windus
LONDON

for Alice

Published in 1990 by
Chatto & Windus Ltd
20 Vauxhall Bridge Road
London SW1V 2SA

821.91

A CIP catalogue record for this book is available from the British Library.

ISBN 0 7011 3595 6

CRA

0701 135 956 1149

ACKNOWLEDGEMENTS

I am grateful to the editors of the following periodicals and
anthologies where some of these poems have appeared: *Adelaide
Review*, *Cencrastus*, *Gairfish*, *Landfall*, *Lines Review*, *London
Magazine*, *London Review of Books*, *Modern Scottish Poetry*, *National
Poetry Competition Prizewinners Anthology 1987*, *New Writing
Scotland*, *Oxford Magazine*, *Oxford Poetry*, *Poetry Review*, *The Times
Literary Supplement*, *Verse*. Some poems were also broadcast on
BBC Radio 3's *Poetry Now* and as a programme in Scottish
Television's *In Verse* series.

Photoset in Linotron Ehrhardt by
Rowland Phototypesetting Ltd, Bury St Edmunds, Suffolk
Printed in Great Britain by
Redwood Press Limited, Melksham, Wiltshire

CONTENTS

'Some people think that the word Nationalism means "let's all put on jackboots and kill everybody else", but our cultural nationalism has a very modest mandate – namely, that we exist. It seems to threaten some people.'

Margaret Atwood,
in *Scotland on Sunday*, 5 February 1989

Opera

Throw all your stagey chandeliers in wheelbarrows and
    move them north
To celebrate my mother's sewing-machine
And her beneath an eighty-watt bulb, pedalling
Iambs on an antique metal footplate
Powering the needle through its regular lines,
Doing her work. To me as a young boy
That was her typewriter. I'd watch
Her hands and feet in unison, or read
Between her calves the wrought-iron letters:
SINGER. Mass-produced polished wood and metal,
It was a powerful instrument. I stared
Hard at its brilliant needle's eye that purred
And shone at night; and then each morning after
I went to work at school, wearing her songs.

The Saltcoats Structuralists

for Douglas Cairns

They found the world's new structure was a binary
Gleaming opposition of two rails

That never crossed but ran on parallel
Straight out of Cairo. From small boys

On Platform One who listened to the great
Schola cantorum of connecting rods

Dreamed-up by Scots-tongued engineers, they went on
To tame the desert, importing locomotives

From a distant Firth. New wives came out, and one,
Shipwrecked off Ailsa Craig, returned to Glasgow,

9

Caught the next boat; her servants had her wardrobe
Replaced in just four hours from the city shops.

Scotsmen among colonial expats
They learned RP, embarrassing their families

In Ayrshire villages where they talked non-stop
About biggah boilahs, crankshawfts. Nicknamed 'The
        Pharaohs',

They never understood the deconstruction
Visited on Empire when their reign in Egypt

Ran out of steam. They first-classed back to Saltcoats,
Post-Nasser; on slow commuter diesels

They passed the bare brick shells of loco-sheds
Like great robbed tombs. They eyed the proud slave faces

Of laid-off engineering workers, lost
In the electronics revolution. Along the prom

They'd holidayed on in childhood, with exotic walking sticks,
History in Residence, they moved

In Sophoclean raincoats. People laughed
At a world still made from girders, an Iron Age

Of Queen Elizabeths, pea-soupers, footplates,
And huge black toilet cisterns named 'St Mungo'.

Kids zapped the videogames in big arcades
Opposite Arran. Local people found

New energy sources, poems didn't rhyme.
The Pharaohs' grandchildren's accents sounded to them

Wee hell-taught ploughmen's. In slow seafront caffs
They felt poststructuralism, tanged with salt.

Bhidhio

They walk towards us in blue overalls, tiny
Millionaires of the rain,

Peat poets, a fiddler with a hacking cough.
They speak what it says on the roadsigns,

But to us always English. Their smiles and glances
Are what gets lost in translation.

After centuries of practising
Australia and Canada, these survivors blockade their lives

Beautifully with abandoned cars and rich
Theological silence. Neighbours

Peg their families' souls on washing lines
In a close surveillance society

Where ministers' noble, orgasmic voices
Say the Evil One is near as he was in Eden

Flying in under the radar. We
Sweep past their bungalows, heading back for the mainland.

They drive slowly to their prayer-meetings, different.
They watch us on their television.

Coll

Imagine an asylum for anemometers,
A discotheque of water.

Horizontal sleet on the west of Coll
Scours the headlands. Tattered crofts
Lie like stone litter that will not rot

On voes and machair. Trespassing through
A frameless window with the wind's white grit
Against me like shot of God's anger

I photograph what I want to show you
Purged of that air. The lens is rainlogged.
My hand is cold to the bone,

But this matters because it sets the limits
All understand. One small lit square,
Chaos made dumb by a window.

Robert Crawford

You're interrupted in the book of the film
By someone ringing who's just seen your name

As the title of an opera. You remember that doctor in
    Mallaig
Born long before Disney and baptised Donald Duck.

What could he have felt? Normality's strange –
Always more of it gets delivered in cartons

With the names washed off. Maybe next century
We'll have extra labels: a noun for the sensation

Of hearing Philip Glass while being driven in a Citroën
Or of sitting down to eat a bag of chips

With two historians of mesmerism near Inverkeithing.
Meantime I'm adjusting to my newfound status

As a matinée for schools. I'm grateful to slip out quietly
By the cellar door and leave myself sometimes

Being private in a deckchair in the garden.

The Only Emperor

He sweated on the running-board. Inside on leather
His business-suited Little Italy cousins

Backed the idea. In summer '31
They put out a contract for an art-deco palace

With raspberry walls. He kept his cool with bad jokes.
Morals were wafer-thin. All that first year

He lived and almost died ice-cream, sold Presbyterian
Salesmen knickerbocker glories; schoolgirls licked
    mountainous cones,

Loving the ones at the top of the range he called
'The Duke of Italy' and 'The Abyssinian'.

A band with epaulettes played waltzes. 'Vanilla Vespers'
Captured the market. Crowds poured in. He moulded

A taste for almond-coating, grated chocolate,
Mixed lime and lemon, strawberry, passion fruits

With a subtle additive that made the waiters
Point out one evening, 'This parlour does not serve

Forces in uniform.' Not a pane of glass
Was left entire. Interned now, he dreamed up

Chilling techniques using bottled gas, new flavours,
And cried internally, unable to stomach

His cousin Giovanni iced by partisans
For taking money sent out from the tills

To do good service. '45, release,
Risorgimento, and the melting away

Of all competitors, their untold stories
Spicing the palace with a sheer mystique

Of old-style limos and men with violins
Customers longed for. The new restaurant

Gave splendid service; heavy electroplated cutlery
Rescued from shipping lines the war had sunk

Brought back good memories. Ex-servicemen took their
      children
And grandchildren to eat *vitello*,

Amused to think their lavish tips might fund
Old-fashioned Neapolitan broadsheets. 'Parmesan!'

Laughter steams-up windows. This St Valentine's Day
The staff are one big family. It's warm

And good to see the groomed tuxedos serving
With part Italian and part local accents

Drawing the blinds with taste, covering up
This small town's finest acreage of glass.

Honeymoon

The photos are as we remembered they would be: huge
Skies swing over the island made of tweed

Like a primary work-pack, teaching us happiness
Isn't colour-coded. Rainlit peaty browns

Bounce back electric as tropicana. Noon
Flicks the beach from fjord to Bahama where the words

Of another scripture start to arrive, beginning
'On the eighth day, after creation was finished,

God began to imagine Luskentyre.'
No more gets written, but the lines still stand as part

Of a plan, the way J. M. Barrie's initials
Scrawled with a diamond on a hotel window are now

Incorporated in its double-glazing. I remember
The days being in mid-flight; we wanted to stroke them

As they grazed past, warmer than starlings. Their
        single-track clarity
Rivals that of emblems, a woman in a cloud

Leans on the shining letters LEX, a man
Jogs towards golden AMOR.

Photographs issue new memories like skateboarders
Round familiar corners – the temple at Eoropie,

The Arnol blackhouse slip back into the light
Of the stainless steel pen in your hand addressing

Thank you letters at the start of our marriage in September.
Let's be like Allan Murchie of Dunfermline

Transported to Australia for wanting a Scottish republic
Who set up a pub called 'The Help Me Thro' the World'.

The Clerk Maxwell Country (*for George Davie*)

Rain in Dumfries, but across the Debatable Lands
Fog clears to his dry talk of electro-

Magnetism. Cybernetics whistles 'Auld Lang Syne',
Storming through thick-walled cottages where science

Means an unusual marriage. Dafty's in his attic
Shifting things round, chairs and classical physics,

At work on the border. His desklight
Burns through storms. A massive fir's blown down

Smashing the gardener's ordered symmetry.
Einstein will come trampling through that gap.

Photonics

We're a new technology, a system that weds
Lasers; no electronics; no gob-drops
Of glass fibre to be teased and spun; just conjugate-phasing
Turning constant signals into rings of light,
A burgh packed with brilliant marriages

Strong the way a towerblock in an earthquake zone
Rocks and quivers, floating erect
On its bed of underground gravels; we're making discoveries
Simplifying, unbuckling at the waist,
Unbuttoning the two pearl buttons at your throat,

Till we lie where the Giant flung his shining Causeway
Over gaunt blue water into these small sweet hills;
We meet as clearly as two beams in a saltire
Bonded at the centre, having each
Come through all the R & D to run on light.

Home

Has canary-yellow curtains, so expensive
At certain times they become unaffordable,
Cost too much patience. A cartoon voice:

'I'm leaving, Elmer.' That's home also, sometimes;
The Eden a person can't go back to. Still . . .
If you don't leave it, it's only a world;

If you never return, just a place like any other.
Home isn't in the *Blue Guide*, the A–Z
I only need for those ten thousand streets

Not one of which has Alice Wales in it.
At home you bolt on the new pine headboard,
Crying. You build from your tears

A hydroponicum; bitter-sweet nutrition
Becomes the address we ripen in like fruit
No one thought would grow here. Home

Is where we hang up our clothes and surnames
Without thought. Home is the instruction: dream home.
An architecture of faint clicks, and smells that haven't yet
        quite.

We grow old in it. Like children, it keeps us young,
Every evening being twenty-one again
With the key in the door, coming back from the library

You're shouting upstairs to me, telling me what you are
In the simplest of words, that I want you to go on repeating
Like a call-sign. You are shouting, 'I'm home.'

Pimpernel

Maybe it was a woman who escaped,
Aged about thirty, joking
She had hair that grew like a hedge.

She mentioned to nobody she was the one.
She turned down the graduate scholarship
Once held by Adam Smith.

Beautiful feet. Her job brought her circulars
Urging the enhancement of macromanagement
For the information resource.

When that language
Made her cry, was it fair
To say yes, it's written like shite?

Nowhere to go, she's the escapee
Who one night rolls over towards you
In bed in a country that hasn't existed

For centuries, whispering, 'I've become a nationalist.'
You can't advise her, now she's your wife,
You listen to her, writing the poems.

The Railway Library

Grass is growing through the disused lines
Of *Marmion* and *Martin Rattler*. You could pick up a book
At any station, racing through its chapters
In a slipcase of steam until your destination
Broke off the story. Rochester met Jane Eyre
At Falkirk High; Bram Stoker's action plunged
Through mile-long tunnels; *The Moonstone* gleamed in
  Paisley.
Women and men bought tickets for good books
That sped home, thundering across the points
Where readers clutched their seats. A suffragette
Sits in her first-class carriage in the cells
Of Monte Cristo; haar and sunlight bleach
High seas off Fife. She vanishes in fog at Leuchars,
Never reads on, still haunted by that picture
Of stone being scraped away and a voice speaking
Through solid wall. Holmes hails a hansom cab
On the poisoner's track in Kelso. Hunched inside
Self-induced personal stereo, sleuthing readers
Read past each other as the four o'clock
Overtakes the mail train, late. Impatient Crewe passengers
For Stevenson are out of luck – his adventures
All borrowed by shy children travelling north
Kidnapped by *Treasure Island*. Books circulate
From Kyle to Wigton; returns, reissued through
First, second, third, get beerstained, reek of cigars.
Some essays outlast viaducts. Folk come
Borrowing words, remembering, misremembering.
After the stock is scrapped, lines uneconomic,
Narratives run unhindered, mothers and daughters
Climb on board, or jump from the moving text
With hankies at their wrists and *Quo Vadis*?

The Dalswinton Enlightenment

Patrick Miller's first iron vessel, the world's
First steamship is swanning across Dalswinton Loch.
A landscape painter, Alexander Naysmith
Perches on deck beside his good friend, Robert Burns.

It's a calm, clear morning. The painter will later invent
The compression rivet, and work out the axial arrangement
Between propeller and engine. The poet will write about the
    light
Of science dawning over Europe, remembering how

Cold sun struck Pat's boat that October day at Dalswinton
When the churning paddles articulated the loch
In triumphant metre, and the locals made some cracks
Almost as if they were watching a ship of fools.

Henry Bell Introduces Europe's First Commercial Steamship

Scanning the universe from Helensburgh
You saw the *Comet* first in your own mind
Remote as Egypt, till it crossed the Firth
Blazing a tail of foam and smoke that seemed

Suddenly normal, the future telescoped
From the other shore. Your Cleopatran dream,
Democratised by Watt's technology
Of fire and air, burned on the water and

Made your name History. Not caring about that
A Glasgow girl at the rail accompanied by
Two sets of radial paddles whistled to her man
Choruses from Allan Ramsay's *The Ever Green*.

Scotland in the 1890s

'I came across these facts which, mixed with others . . .'
Thinking of Helensburgh, J. G. Frazer
Revises flayings and human sacrifice;
Abo of the Celtic Twilight, St Andrew Lang
Posts him a ten-page note on totemism
And a coloured fairy book – an Oxford man
From Selkirk, he translates Homer in his sleep.

'When you've lived here, even for a short time,
Samoa's a bit like Scotland – there's the sea . . .
Back in Auld Reekie with a pen that sputtered
I wrote my ballad, "Ticonderoga" or
"A Legend of the West Highlands", then returned
To King Kalakaua's beach and torches –
You know my grandfather lit Lismore's south end?'

Mr Carnegie has bought Skibo Castle.
His union jack's sewn to the stars and stripes.
James Murray combs the dialect from his beard
And files slips for his massive *Dictionary*.
Closing a fine biography of mother,
Remembering Dumfries, and liking boys,
James Barrie, caught in pregnant London silence,
Begins to conceive the Never Never Land.

John Logie Baird

When it rained past Dumbarton Rock
You skipped Classics for a motorbike exploration

Of the Clyde's slow Raj. In sodden memsahibs' gardens
Hydrangeas unfurled into fibre-optics.

A dominie lochgellied you once
For pronouncing 'Eelensburgh' like those wild, untouchable
    tinks

Who, if they could see your biker's career from today's
Long distance, would snigger. A socialist most famous for

Inventing an undersock, screened from douce cousins,
Under bamboos at a small jam factory

Near Port of Spain you achieved television
And paid for it. At the trials a boy called Reith

Risen from your old class shook hands, then wrote you off.
You worked. When World War II ended

Baird equipment broadcast victory in the Savoy
But not one diner said cheerio when you faded,

An obsolete wallah, edited out, still beaming
One hand outstretched across those Clydelike waves.

Man of Vision

for Stephen Conroy

In your painting from Logie Baird's birthplace
A bareskinned man, arm raised, adjusts a movie
Projector's lens. It is pointed towards us, so we
Are what is being shown. He is getting us into focus.

Only a trick of perspective. It's just
A game to think we are linked to him and he
To the light source, which is far behind those gestures
He broadcasts with his fingers, twitching shadow pictures

We can't see – the nervous ears of a rabbit,
A mouth with silhouette lips unreadably
Tempting us to narrate. It's a silent picture.
The seated clothed man has turned his back, intent on his
     papers.

We're the ones faced with the standing figure whose clothes
Slip from him, the man of vision
We're trying to unravel. He will soon be nude, an eccentric
Who takes a white nipple of light in his fingers, testing it

Always in full view. He is potent
As basic integers – 1, 2, 3, 4, 5, 6, 7 – a daring
Remake of the Statue of Liberty, the Light of the World
In Helensburgh with a comet's naked eye.

Beloved

Along from Helensburgh, under the unthinkable hills
Are silos. The peninsulas' prongs
Accept sunset like a dubious blessing.

A thousand mediocre landscape painters
Have botched this low light gilding the water, its slow
Turneresque burning-away.

Birdwatchers train their priestly binoculars
Round Rosneath Point over birches and brambles.
The superpowers are aware of Glen Fruin.

Syrophenician

You were the Syrophenician woman
Arguing with God, a dog among the Jews.
Glare islanded and baked you, shadows turned

On your crazy daughter. Border squatter
Between yes and no, you persisted, stubborn bitch
Till your answer ripened, like the nod to Zacchaeus in his
    tree

Or Loch Lomond light stunning a houseboat's windows
Into juddery polythene, a whiteout moment
When the one whom you loved most was healed.

Fiesta

Maybe inevitable, it's not as expected, like grandeur
Coming in cans or Stevenson sailing to Samoa
From his Edinburgh childhood. Those lorry convoys stowed
  with sheet-music
And philharmonias to play it stockpiled for Life's Great
  Occasions
Couldn't cram up this B road beside the Water of Tig.
You remotor to places that happily bored you in childhood –
They're the same, different: the next stitch in lacemaking
  and then
The one after. Ayrshire's a mud database
Updated hourly by jets into Prestwick
Or news items dialled into conservation villages
That urge Please Drive Slowly in case you miss them
  completely;
Someone's scrawled FUCKING LYRICAL, these
  Scotlands running together
In what's simply this evening with pheasants flying through
  reports
On the postmodern condition and a seamist at Ballantrae.
Pubs old as tea-dances key their accounts
Into microcomputers; Robert Burns's House of Statues
  opens
On to a Ladies and Gents; bracken
Sparks through the words. Returning, there's a snell east
  wind
And a need to love it, fir trees sleeking the windscreen
Like the green spines of Thackeray, happy.

Inner Glasgow

You were a small red coat among the pit bings
That aren't there now, between Cambuslang
And Shettleston, with *Tell Me Why*, *Look and Learn*;

The quays have altered, liners replaced by jasmine;
Where docks are cultivated, hard nostalgia
Steam-rivets us to ghosts we love, in murals

Where everybody looks the same and sings
Of oppression, smokes, drinks lager, shouts out 'fuck'.
Shops sell us. Entrepreneurs' industrial

Museums postcard grime; we're pseudo-Griersonned.
But you refuse these foisted images, stay
Too true, still here, grown up in your red coat.

My inner Glasgow, you don't leave me, I
Do not leave you. A tubular steel frontage, roadcones
Flash towards us like the tiny folded pictures

In pop-up books, the lovely, lovely details
Too close to label art, that bring on laughter
When words cut out their starter motor, leaving us

Idling beside a cloudless firth. Those shorelights
Spread beyond Millport, beckon us to marry,
To lie along the bowsprits of our lives.

Seuils

An early morning windowcleaner tunes his radio.
Its French songs don't mist the glass. Couples

Who last night opened themselves like books
Speed up through the foreign lyrics filling

This pedestrian precinct in between
Sleeping together and officework.

Feeling for calculators inside breast pockets
They check their keys. The days are getting longer,

Squeezing the nights. For young people in May
Glasgow is a huge anthology of prefaces.

'Let me introduce you . . .' Sunlit streets run on forever,
Though everything that opens gets shut up too

Till next morning or evening – megastores, discotheques,
        foreplay –
And hovering at the back of it, mercury behind a mirror,

Are threshold demons, an old man playing a piccolo
Night after night in Nelson Mandela Place.

A Saying

I'm calling you late in the evening, calling
Over hundreds of miles, you cannot hear me yet.

I'm calling you by a public name, a number;
Pushing the buttons. Roundabouts will be lit

By East Kilbride headlights, Polo Mint City they call it
Familiarly spinning its human rings of cars.

Through the machine I hear your Glasgow accent,
Your voiceprint. I just called, to say.

Cambuslang

My childhood passes on a bicycle
Down West Coats Road, beneath our sycamore
That filters July sunlight through the slow
Sidereal quiet of the suburb

Where my father calls our garden 'the croft', and grows
Rows of potatoes, a countryman Glasgow disguised
Too long as a bank teller. A piece of broken glass
Shines on the lawn. Something always glistens

In the yards of grass that gently separate
A small boy from this same house where my parents
Live on together, smiling just beyond
The flowers-only gardens, the conservation area.

Détente

The Chief in tails spends the long coniferous evening
Walking with the Field Marshal. They trail their macs on
    the pineneedles.

Central heating has failed in the motel cabins, but nobody
Dare interrupt. Reporters

Bristle with flashbulbs, impatient as grounded jets.
This accord will be nicknamed *A Night at the Opera*.

Dark limousines are revving up
For the drive back to different worlds.

Dialogue

In the trailer-park two trailers are drawn up back to back, each coupled to a lorry cab. A single polished wooden chair sits on the end of each trailer. The chairs face one another. The two friends

sit on the chairs and start talking about the state of their country, remembering their childhoods, and hopes there had been then of a remedy. Sometimes the two friends

agree, sometimes they differ strongly. As they share a packet of biscuits, solutions emerge, a plan of action. Then the lorries rev up, move off. A widening gap appears between the chairs, but the two friends

stay seated, go on talking, though by now one lorry is winding into the northern uplands, the other accelerating far south. The two friends

speak simultaneously, often brilliantly. Occasionally messengers in cars drive at high speed from one to the other with tapes and shorthand transcriptions but the conversation remains out of sync, however much the two friends

do not want it to be so. This was a long time ago. Now there are only two empty chairs (one in a north-east fishing village, the other in a southern pedestrian-precinct) facing each other. When people see either chair they walk forward to read the inscription. Each chair is called *The Two Friends*.

The Approach

Floating, floating. In the tall dairy
Of the floods beyond, ruled with a grid of days,
Pigeons call. You remain like honey
Approaching through the hinterland, with deer abrupt
In front of the headlamps. You can absorb
Long novels of sleep and thermocouples
As the waves crash in. Night lowers its landing gear
And turns on one side. Over the telephone
Yesterday may be recounted.
Evening brindles, waiting outside the church
Pine smells blend with the scent of cooked food.
What time is it? Like oystercatchers, breath
On the flutehole quickens us, makes us persist;
It is approaching in boatsongs, it is approaching
With loyalty running in new shoes
Through a soaking meadow, pollen-drift
Sloughed off on your bare knees.
Each of us has the laser on the disc's rotation
Dispensing arias, zither's, moon-shaped lute's.
Feathered with a tang of salt, it approaches
Floating, about to be:
Ours, when the time is proper, silent
At the sea's edge, and the surf breeze brings you
Laughing ashore from the Gulf Stream at Machrihanish.

Thai Horses

On your left breast the blue Thai horse
Champs in lacquer. Our train heads north
Where milky air holds the hill passes

With a lit haar. Resisting that
Is a kind of love: to look Glasgow straight in the face
Being alien, and taken in

Warily. Let that army of dribbling ghosts
Die. Crossing the border
Where bog myrtle drifts its smell beside

A single riverboat, we become multiplied
And irresistible, a thousand blue
Thai horses at the gate of Scotland.

Kyoto

The peats stagger over the long brown cut. June
So hot that blue horses
Drift from the stained glass into the loch, Rannoch Moor
Hard as concrete. The ferry goes back and forward
Like a few simple cards reshuffled.
Crossing to the island, dragged through green water,
    crossing back.
90 in the shade. The longest day.
You could see to Kyoto
If you leant your head on my elbow.

Nec Tamen Consumebatur

The most famous violinist on Eigg,
Denounced from the pulpit for his Gaelic folksongs,

Threw on the fire an instrument made
By a pupil of Stradivarius.

'The sooner,' thundered *The Times*,
'All Welsh specialities disappear

From the face of the earth the better.'
You whose parents came from a valley

North of Hanoi are now living in Princeton
Teaching low-temperature physics. Often

When you spoke about poems in Vietnamese
I heard behind the pride in your voice

Like a ceilidh in an unexpected place
The burning violins of small peoples.

On the Way Home
Che-Lan-Vien

On a clear day I abandoned the city
To go back to the mountains of the race called Hoi.

Their towers were here, gone thin with waiting,
Temples eroded under long rain.
Deserted, the river dragged in shadow. Statues
Whimpered at their open blisters.

At evening, surrounded by bending treetops,
Crowds of blind spirits linked their hands
To grope through the forest. Shadows dissolved in chaos,
Waves of scent fluttered with the sound of farewells.

Battlesites. The souls of warriors screamed
And the blood of the Cham flowed over days,
Over months of angry injustice. Cham bones
Do not stop rustling. But there was peace once

In the country of Chiem, yellow hamlets
Coloured by afternoon, young girls
Gone back to their village in rose-coloured dresses
That billowed over speech and laughter.

Palaces glinted in sunlight under
An open sky, a boat lay dreaming
On the still river, and beside that tower
The sacred elephants meditated together.

Evening was milky. In a light like glass or jade
The court of Chiem gazed at ivory skins
Of Chiem girls whose dreams were the song of flutes,
Their music the sway of their bodies.

I met these things on the journey home.
Days and months pass. They will not leave me.
I cannot free myself from the sadness,
The regret for the race of Hoi.

Translated from the Vietnamese by Mai-Lan and Robert Crawford.

*CHE-LAN-VIEN (b. 1920), though not of the Chiem-thanh people
(also known as Hoi), took up their cause and wrote poetry about their
plight, similar to that of the American Indians. At the time of his
writing, Hoi architecture remained only as ruins and their descen-
dants had retreated to live in the hills, after the conquest of their land
in the south of Viet-Nam.*

Whistling Willie, Donside 1928

Two boys took him an ounce
Of Pop's best tobacco. He talked

About sheep, cricket, and Hampshire; slept
On a steep bracken bank behind the sixteen-stall stable

Fingering his tin pipe, never asking,
Till my grandmother thought he should move inside

The last stall. She cooked him an evening meal
Of salmon, neeps, and fresh spuds.

Pop carried engraved silver condiments
Out on a tray to the straw:

'Cannae gie an Englishman his dinner
Wi'oot the pepper an saut.'

Dunoon

Mist becomes polythene we burst with our fingers.
Along the coastline hills are wrapped up.
Tomatoes, leeks. The country is on a level with these things.
Tugging our cold thumbs,

Petulantly pleading, love
Cannot replace shopping or the mending of telephones.
Accelerating away, behind tinted windows,
The chairman drafts a long letter.

Iona

Doctor Johnson feels seasick. The small man who
As the years twitch past will slowly overtake him
Has gone off to scrabble for green stones.

Those bearded boatmen who rowed him here
Mutter in Gaelic. Johnson noticed their powder-red eyes
When they offered him oatmeal. He likes them

Knowing all along their abbey is full of pigshit;
This place of beginnings is cold, bare, muddy.
He is starting to get tired of London.

Remote

Ignorant of gas, they locked themselves
Indoors and suffocated. Cows dropped in the fields.
'We thought that factory made medicine.'

Girls rub eyes sore with videotape, slouch out
To stare at big, unedited clouds.
It'll rain tonight. There's shopping to be done.

Use the remote to fast-rewind rough hands
Reaching through leaves, then replace the cassette.
What has that stuff to do with being nice

To Ken and Eileen's kid who's not quite there?
Turn off the studio's main lights. Go home.
Time Magazine. The National Geographic.

Mr and Mrs William Mulock in the Museum of Ethnology

Mr Mulock, staring at
The gaps between the hieroglyphs,
Shuffles his feet, and wonders what
His wife sees in that row of stiffs

Embalmed in old stone coffins. She
Is rapturous, 'The guide book said,
"All visitors must go and see
The fertile Nile's immortal dead"

And now we have.' The husband coughs
But smiles to please his cultured wife;
Lost in the Pharaohs' autographs,
She disregards a common life.

Woman and man, each stands and seems
Odd, undeciphered, quite alone,
Surrounded by elusive dreams,
Fragments of the Rosetta Stone.

Native questions

Ghosts with lightning eyes, peeled
Aboriginal corpses

Gather insects through imported gloaming
Catechised in Auld Kirk Gaelic.

After Culloden this land was possessed,
Settled in a trance of cash.

Mraat, ghosts with interrogating eyes,
Go walkabout in Caledonia Australis.

Transformer

Lengths of model railway track jutted from the Pictish stones.
When I bent down to look at a horseman's head or at the comb
and mirror, scale-model engines hurtled towards me. *Ivanhoe*,
The Lady of the Lake, *The Fair Maid of Perth* with gleaming
pistons – I had to catch them or they'd shoot off the ends of
their tracks. I lurched from stone to stone, grabbing them. In
the darkness they slackened off. At midnight I wrapped the
locomotives in plastic bags to carry them away; their metal
bodies grew heavy and cold as I walked. Home, I laid them in
the loft, peering at them, wondering if they'd work on my
layout. That night I saw them carved new, crewed by warriors,
steaming their way into battle. At Aberlemno model replica
carriages with Victorian coachwork lay in the grass, unspotted.
Mist was perforated with cries and grinding metal. *Royal Scots*
poured from the stones.

Scotland

Glebe of water, country of thighs and watermelons
In seeded red slices, bitten by a firthline edged
With colonies of skypointing gannets,
You run like fresh paint under August rain.

It is you I return to, mouth of erotic Carnoustie,
Edinburgh in helio. I pass like an insect
Among shoots of ferns, gloved with pollen, intent
On listing your meadows, your pastoral Ayrshires, your glens

Gridded with light. A whey of meeting
Showers itself through us, sluiced from defensive umbrellas.
Running its way down raincoat linings, it beads
Soft skin beneath. A downpour takes us

At the height of summer, and when it is finished
Bell heather shines to the roots,
Belly-clouds cover the bings and slate cliffs,
Intimate grasses blur with August rain.

Scotland

Semiconductor country, land crammed with intimate
    expanses,
Your cities are superlattices, heterojunctive
Graphed from the air, your cropmarked farmlands
Are epitaxies of tweed.

All night motorways carry your signal, swept
To East Kilbride or Dunfermline. A brightness off low
    headlands
Beams-in the dawn to Fife's interstices,
Optoelectronics of hay.

Micro-nation. So small you cannot be forgotten,
Bible inscribed on a ricegrain, hi-tech's key
Locked into the earth, your televised Glasgows
Are broadcast in Rio. Among circuitboard crowsteps

To be miniaturised is not small-minded.
To love you needs more details than the Book of Kells –
Your harbours, your photography, your democratic intellect
Still boundless, chip of a nation.

A Scottish Assembly

Circuitry's electronic tartan, the sea,
Libraries, fields – I want the lot

To fly off and scatter, but most of all
Always to come home to roost

In this unkempt country where a handicapped printer,
Engraver of dog collars, began with his friends

The ultimate encyclopedia.
Don't expect any rhyme or reason

For Scotland remaining an explosion reversed
Or ordinariness a fruited vine

Or why I came back here to choose my union
On the side of the ayes, remaining a part

Of this diverse assembly – Benbecula, Glasgow, Bow of
    Fife –
Voting with my feet, and this hand.

Edinburgh

My capital of sulking jewels
Misinvested, glimmers through the haar.
Under it, horsehair sofas, quaichs
And portrait heads in museum store-tunnels
Furnish the salons of an independent
Doppelgänger-townscape, locked.

Above ground, councillors start to debate
Charging admission to the city.
An occasional tubelit attendant
Visits that undernation where every item
Has its provenance label, an accurate pawnticket
Ready in case of redemption.

Robert Frost at Kingsbarns

Granaries of well-dressed stone, straight from the ballads
Hunch round a village. Over there
Just sea and barley. One tall man strides out

Through afternoon, hot silence thick enough
To spread on oatcakes; Scotland, mother's country,
Few tourists, red tiled roofs, authentic sea.

He lies down in a cowfield, lolling back
Like an old print of a Caledonian shepherd,
Escaped from that wandered prof up at St Andrews

Who's inventing Fife's own palaeolithic sites.
The rich soil warms, Frost sees America
Among the multimillion sheaves of barley.

Sir David Brewster Invents the Kaleidoscope

He clears the atmosphere of cool St Andrews –
Into dense constellations that revolve
At a hand's turn. From Aberdeen, Lord Byron
Looks on with half of Europe, starry-eyed.
Baudelaire will say modern art's like this
Brilliant and shifty, a fantastic model
Of how the real will open up, the micro-
Particular, the split, then the expanding
Universe that spills out silent stars
Light years from Scotland. It's a toy –
No copyright, it made the man who made it
No money. Just a universal sold
In Glasgow or Bangkok. With an English friend
Later he helped invent the camera,
Became a friend of Hill and Adamson
Who set up tripods in Fife villages,
Went back to being local, became fact.

The Minister's Marriage

Snowed-in for months with God and a model railway
That snaked round the lounge, he married a rich woman.

It was she who extended the manse
To hold more stations, a level crossing, sheds

For new locomotives, her wedding gift
Suddenly doubling the kingdom.

Through bleak midwinter in an earthfloored kitchen
The *Flying Scotsman* was never late.

One Sunday he preached the perfect sermon
About Stephenson's *Rocket*. Mostly, they did little talking.

Whenever he entered a room full of silences
He always knew which one to pick.

Bedroom

Across the firth at dusk from the Kilmacolm road
Come stalks of light. The one bank touches the other.
A mica evening. Greenock signals across

To a window high on the Hill House. Instead of curtains
White wooden shutters ready to be fastened

Going to bed. That room's a museum now
Pale with chinoiserie beyond the harling.
Nobody dreams there. Everybody does.

La Bibliothèque de Nora Barnacle

I.m. Richard and Mary Ellmann

I liked the look of him at Finn's Hotel.
A writer. Cut no ice with me. Thin hands.
Should've been a counter-tenor – made my name
Never sound ugly. Knew I'd be the one

To treat him just like any other man
Letting him write. And now he's dead no need
To read his stuff. You do that if you want.
I've got them in my room, all my own books.

Rain

A motorbike breaks down near Sanna in torrential rain,
Pouring loud enough to perforate limousines, long enough
To wash us to Belize. Partick's
Fish-scaled with wetness. Drips shower from foliage,
    cobbles, tourists
From New York and Düsseldorf at the tideline
Shoes lost in bogs, soaked in potholes, clarted with glaur.
An old woman is splashed by a bus. A gash
In cloud. Indians
Arrived this week to join their families and who do not feel
Scottish one inch push onwards into a drizzle
That gets heavy and vertical. Golf umbrellas
Come up like orchids on fast-forward film; exotic
Cagoules fluoresce nowhere, speckling a hillside, and
                                           plump
Off dykes and gutters, overflowing
Ditches, a granary of water drenches the shoulders
Of Goatfell and Schiehallion. Maps under perspex go
    bleary,
Spectacles clog, Strathclyde, Tayside, Dundee
Catch it, fingers spilling with water, oil-stained
As it comes down in sheets, blows
Where there are no trees, snow-wet, without thought of the
    morrow.
Weddings, prunes, abattoirs, strippers, Glen Nevis, snails
Blur in its democracy, down your back, on your breasts.
In Kilmarnock a child walks naked. A woman laughs.
In cars, in Tiree bedrooms, in caravans and tenements,
Couples sleeved in love, the gibbous Govan rain.

The Great McEwen, Scottish Hypnotist

The Man Who Made the Sphinx Laugh, The Great
    McEwen
Shook down South Island like a thunderstorm.
Decked out with huge Scots thistles, posters show
Vacant-eyed bankers standing on a debutante
Suspended between chairs. In chequered tweeds
A portly dandy, posing legs apart,
Plants one well-polished shoe on each robed breast.
The girl swoons backwards in delicious cotton
Without pain, holding Dunedin breathless
As the Stupendous Cataleptic Test
Reaches its climax. Morning-suited,
McEwen bows, half Transylvanian, half
Kirk elder, far too woodenly impressive
Not to impress us in our century
Which conjured ANZAC northwards to resist
The great dictators' mesmerised mass rallies.
We smirk at his vast claims, but want the vision
Of calculated innocence that fired him
Half round the world to a crammed New Zealand hall
To captivate it, singing 'The Flowers of the Forest'
Then standing quiet, white-cuffed wrists extended
Like a politician's, leading, levitating
Up from the sawdust floor of history
A rapt small country that was not his own.

The People's Palace

Built of red sandstone on the bleaching green,
Our common ground on which James Watt invented
His separate condenser, it contains
A Winter Gardens in an upside-down
Ship's hull of glass; inside, sheer Scots Australia.
Councillor Robert Crawford spoke for it.

Less grandiose than the Great Hall of the People, less *bijou*
Than Windsor, it is about the royalty
Of laundresses and electricians. Calton weavers
Bankrupted a textile merchant who privatised
Part of this place. Clyde waters swept away
All sign of what he did. The People's Palace,

Victoriana, po-faced as a fridge,
Freezes the anarchy from which things grew:
Oak boxes lined with velvet from Culloden,
The Word, *The Clincher*, voices of the urban,
Classic Adam mouldings, a stool where Wesley stood,
Disaster Bibles, rubbed communion tokens –

To all of these I'm returning to be married
Into the uncrowned with their grate tradition
Fired up again. We'll burn and then we'll water
A university of grass, downtrodden, dancing
In quadrilles beneath streetlights. A Fiesta at Charing Cross
Accelerates under the chandeliers of the rain.

Alba Einstein

When proof of Einstein's Glaswegian birth
First hit the media everything else was dropped:
Logie Baird, Dundee painters, David Hume – all
Got the big E. Physics documentaries
Became peak-viewing; Scots publishers hurled awa
MacDiarmid like an overbaked potato, and swooped
On the memorabilia: *Einstein Used My Fruitshop*,
Einstein in Old Postcards, Einstein's Bearsden Relatives.
Hot on their heels came the A. E. Fun Park,
Quantum Court, Glen Einstein Highland Malt.
Glasgow was booming. Scotland rose to its feet
At Albert Suppers where The Toast to the General Theory
Was given by footballers, panto-dames, or restaurateurs.
In the US an ageing lab-technician recorded
How the Great Man when excited showed a telltale glottal
    stop.
He'd loved fiddlers' rallies. His favourite sport was curling.
Thanks to this, Scottish business expanded
Endlessly. His head grew toby-jug-shaped,
Ideal for keyrings. He'd always worn brogues.
Ate bannocks in exile. As a wee boy he'd read *The Beano*.
His name brought new energy: our culture was solidly based
On pride in our hero, The Universal Scot.

Tradition and the Individual Talent
for W. N. Herbert

It flits, translated like Ossian's poems
From originals somehow reported missing

Without being recorded. One year before Wilbur and
    Orville,
Secure above firwoods, a silvery dream of a biplane

Loops the loop through the Carse of Gowrie.
Engine-drone pibroch comes down to land

Among a billion needles. A young man walks

On that forest floor carpet, years after his death,
Back to our era, his chainstore raincoat

Reeking of fuel-oil, ears alert
For the rhythm of a rising propeller.

Apertures

The divorcé who photographed doors
Bored us to tears, opening up

His hobby of half a lifetime.
No two were alike: that coarsegrained barndoor in Iowa

Sagging a little, a drayman's entrance in Norfolk
Open and shut, each with its enormous story,

Aperçus, taken too far.
Then, at last, at the end of the album,

A small dark gap from which he had peeled
The apartment door that used to be his.

Souvenir of Scunthorpe

after the painting by Gordon Hendry

You were the Scots girl in the class, your breasts
Accented in a shapeless cardigan,

School uniform. Even then we knew
You were one of a kind, the kind that grows to be

Nobody's secretary. Your red hair
Scalded my memory. When I look at you

Pert, alert, and framed holding a pencil
Marked 'Souvenir of Scunthorpe', you're not only

A painted prefect scenting independence
But someone like her, and the book you're reading

Ceases to be *The Prime of Miss Jean Brodie*.
It starts to change into the one I made

My early life of, drafted out in Glasgow.
'Reader, I married her,' the sequel starts.

Ossianic Fragments

It's rumoured in Rotary circles that uranium's been
    discovered in the shrunken heads
Of Fiona Macleod. Bonnie Prince Charlie's
Broken out again with Jeanie Deans and Mendelssohn
But we're trying to control things. They're disguised as one
    another.

Already we've rounded up a lot of the landscape, but only
Because the mountains kept getting themselves in the wrong
    order
And so were caught out. We had good maps. The financial
    and anthropological implications of all this
Could be catastrophic. Professors J. MacDougall Hay and
    D. K. Broster

Have been called in as consultants on the question of the
    infrastructure
Of *Roamin' in the Gloamin'*. They're convinced these
    Hebrides could still constitute
An advanced geotechnology if they set their mind to it,
But there's still near-hysteria over those gelid scotch pies.

It's all in my report with the Lochailort coefficients and –
Oh, forget it. We've a free factsheet about how
To be abducted familiarly through an interwar remake
Billowing under a 40-watt Celtic Twilight that's curtained
    the Solway

In a haar brimming with small print from the notes at the
    back of *Redgauntlet*.
If you get into trouble, hum the tune of *Dark Clouds*
Weave their New Tartan Ribbons in the High Bald Hair of the
    Cuillins.
Those kyles are so sadly non-viable.

The Scottish National Cushion Survey

Our heritage of Scottish cushions is dying.
Teams of careful young people on training schemes
Arrived through a government incentive, counting
Every cushion. In Saltcoats, through frosty Lanark.
They even searched round Callanish
For any they'd missed. There are no more Scottish cushions
Lamented the papers. Photographs appeared
Of the last cushion found in Gaeldom.
Silk cushions, pin cushions, pulpit cushions.
We must preserve our inheritance.
So the museums were built: The Palace of Cushions, the
     National
Museum of Soft Seating, and life went on elsewhere
Outside Scotland. The final Addendum was published
Of *Omnes Pulvini Caledonii.*
Drama documentaries. A chapter closed.
And silently in Glasgow quick hands began
Angrily making cushions.

Truth

Mining it employs so many folk
Who're awkward and uncouth;
Naturally people make
Economies with the truth

Because the whole industry's out of date,
Needs to be revamped
On the covers of mags, and mags can't wait
For news to be rubber-stamped.

Home truths don't sell. We need a big T
Marketed like a leading brand
With a catchy name – 'William Wallace' or 'Key' –
Easy to understand.

Commuters from the Cotswolds, Surrey and Hove
Voted for it in a booth.
Only extremists now could love
Scotland more than The Truth.

Tweeds

Ready-to-wear moors, their darker straths
Playgrounds for erotic picnics;

Evenings scented with sphagnum moss,
Secret, pollen-speckled grass;

When dawn comes people will say they've heard
Birdsong rise from our clothing.

Cycle

A city the size of Manchester
Stops. Reporters listen at basements.
Nobody takes in the washing.

Eardley's at her easel on top of a cliff
At Catterline, behind her
Teatowels whipped by the wind.

This Christmas taking our clothes from the dryer
I kneel at its round door, pulling them through
Bundled together, still warm.

Experiments

Engineers are munching toadfruit
With Ovid Surprize. A duck barks. It's lunch.
'I hear he put her hand right into her jeans.'
'They went from the typing pool into the bank.'

Peaceful. Only the mewing of cattle
On an idyllic English Wednesday.
But the horse weeps, lying under the coffee-table;
'They hate me because I am human.'

Anthropology

We could stay on. The wallpaper watched
With its hundred eyes. 'Your funding has been renewed.'

I was given chocolates by the shopgirl who hid
Her protruding jaw, and smiled as if she were mother.

Father showed me his scrapbook bulging with photographs
    of ears.
New specimens were delivered by train.

At night longbearded moneylenders, miles away,
Funnelled their prayers through my bedroom wall.

The Land o' Cakes

Bens ran with venison. Green straths ripened with grouse.
In the Highlands people didn't use knives and forks. They
    were cleared like a table
To make way for shortbread. The Grampians got packed in
    tins.
Study-holidays with napkins and geological hammers
Chipped bits away. The most bestial lay right down
On the naked ground and grazed, the polite
Would point to a landmark, then ask their gillies
To go over and cut a few slices. Loch Lomond
Intoxicated Europe. Bottling plants jammed the glens.
Oatmeal, Castle Rock, scones and bannocks
Soon accounted for most of Lothian, but some parts were
    inedible.
Districts of Dundee defied food science
And had to be fed to pigs. Glasgow
Until recently was thought emetic. It has begun to be
    swallowed,
But always New York State enjoyed the better cuts: Ben
    Nevis,
Lismore, Glen Luss. After the clubhouse feast,
History lies back, stout as John Bull
Bursting through his waistcoat. Soya for us,
The trite menu says in its tartanette cover,
The tender parts have all been eaten.

Balancing

Up beat, up beat, topiaried bludgeons
Try to cull Glasgow or Freetown shouts,
Repeating that they sound so cute.

Elocutionists hover like cat doctors
Whose body heat brings out invisible ink
On laundered shirtfronts: ETON & OXFORD YA
    BASS.

We learn to live with merchant bankers.
Their vowels lope down their tongues' red carpets.
Their wives uncover bruises.

From a dream of Celtic and Orange Lodges, Odysseus
Took a red hot olive branch out of the ash
To drive through the Cyclops's eye.

Rep

Fed up all day shouting through door-entry systems
Signalling through double-glazing

You just have to phone and ask what this new programme
    means.
'Hi, I'm not here just now; if you leave your name

And number after the tone, I'll get back as soon as I can.'
Even the office photocopier

Has a value-free accent, 'Remember to remove the original.'
Complaints all bring back Personnel's

REPRESENTATIONS ARE BEING MADE ON
    YOUR BEHALF
So you think about weekends, tubes of colour,

Your unfinished portrait; that rich, small palette,
Varnishing it with linseed oil.

Starter

In August the Braes are soused with beech nuts.
Taped music dribbles from cruising ice-cream vans
Sweet and banal as raspberry.

Off bracken on the slope above Castlemilk
Imagination hang-glides out over Glasgow –
I launch some grandly abstract nouns,

Beginning, Risorgimento,
Platting them in an incessant vision-poem,
My multimillion bar Bolero

Till I turn away towards the woods of Cathkin
Where your slim, silhouetted figure, head cocked,
Stands like the numeral 1.